# Table of Contents




Rourke Educational Media
A Division of Carson Dellosa Education
rourkeeducationalmedia.com

# Can you find these words?

coach

gi

mat

roll

# Let's Train!

I train jiu-jitsu.

I wear a **gi.**

I wear a belt.

I practice jiu-jitsu with my **coach**.

I practice with my class.

We practice our skills on a **mat**.

It is soft to protect us.

It's time to compete!

The timer starts. I **roll** with my friends.

Sometimes I win.
Sometimes I lose.

I always learn. I always have fun!

# Did you find these words?

I practice jiu-jitsu with my **coach**.

I wear a **gi**.

We practice our skills on a **mat**.

I **roll** with my friends.

# Photo Glossary

**coach** (kohch): A person who teaches and trains athletes.

**gi** (gee): A two-piece white garment worn in jiu-jitsu and other martial arts.

**mat** (mat): A large, thick floor pad used to protect athletes.

**roll** (rohl): A term that means to grapple or spar in jiu-jitsu. The goal is to get your opponent to submit.

# Index



## About the Author

Barry Cole lives in sunny Florida and enjoys living a healthy lifestyle along with his five-year-old son, Brody. His interests include jiu-jitsu, running, boating, and anything outdoors.



www.rourkeeducationalmedia.com

PHOTO CREDITS: Cover ©attl; Pg 2, 4, 15, 15 ©FatCamera; Pg 2, 6, 14, 15 ©kali9; Pg 2, 8, 14, 15 ©kali9; Pg 2, 11, 14, 15 ©kali9; Pg 3 ©FatCamera; Pg 10 ©kali9; Pg 12 ©FatCamera

Edited by: Kim Thompson
Cover and interior design by: Rhea Magaro-Wallace

**Library of Congress PCN Data**
Jiu-Jitsu / Barry Cole
(Ready for Sports)
ISBN 978-1-73160-412-5 (hard cover)(alk. paper)
ISBN 978-1-73160-418-7 (soft cover)
ISBN 978-1-73160-632-7 (e-Book)
ISBN 978-1-73160-655-6 (ePub)
Library of Congress Control Number: 2018967359

Printed in the United States of America,
North Mankato, Minnesota